The Old Wolf

and

Jack and the Beanstalk

Reading Practice with *Ellie's Code*
Level 3

By

ELIANA VILLARROEL

Illustrated by

Mauricio Sanchez-Patzy & Victoria Jimenez

Text and illustrations copyright © 2008 by Eliana Villarroel

All rights reserved. No part of this book may be reproduced or utilized in any form or by any means, electronic or mechanical, including photocopying, recording, or by any information storage or retrieval system without written permission from the author.

ISBN 978-0-9911507-5-5

Summary and Directions:

The research-based method used in Ellie's Code is designed to teach children and older non-readers, including those with reading and spelling difficulties, learning disabilities, and English language learners, to decode, build fluency, and develop spelling accuracy.

Color-coded words aid and guide the brain to recognize mini-words within words and spelling patterns to process faster. This develops automaticity leading to greater fluency.

Using this color-coded method allows the reader to discover a unique, simple method to decode and spell the English language with ease and enjoyment.

Old Wolf's adventures in his quest to help Jack and his mother hold the reader's attention and interest. There is humor in Old Wolf's unique sense of ingenuity which delights the reader when he finds obstacles along his path and manages to find creative solutions to overcome them. On his long journey, he runs into some characters that either help him, or create more problems. Being an old wolf, he is at times confused, or pleasantly surprised by the new technological gadgets which help him communicate with old friends and find his way to Jack's house.

This Level 3 story is recommended for third through fifth grade level students. *Old Wolf's Search for Pinocchio* is a Level 4 color-coded sequel story with a higher vocabulary level recommended to improve reading fluency.

For eight years, this method was thoroughly tested and successfully used with hundreds of special education students, English language learners, and students who were identified at risk because of their inability to read and write at grade level.

After approximately 30 hours of instruction, the average reading fluency growth had an increase of 39 words per minute. Grade level reading fluency tests with black text were used to determine progress. All participants came from first through fifth grade levels. Students who participated in the program were first identified as being far below basic or below basic in reading fluency. Students made an easy transition from the color-coded material to all black text.

SUMMARY GUIDE FOR COLOR-CODE USAGE:

COLOR CODE:	USE:	SAMPLES:
BLUE LETTER (S)	- Identify whole words or mini-words within word(s) and/or spelling patterns which can be easily decoded in isolation.	as, fast, has, all, call, can, the, them, for, only, just, think, story, together, watch, you, before,
GREEN LETTER (S)	- Complete all the sounds required to decode the word when added to the blue letters and/or the blue and red letters.	they, was, about, maybe, words, ants
	- May serve to identify the change of nouns from singular to plural.	legs, pigs, bricks
	- Regular verb-tense endings: (present progressive, past tense)	doing, falling, saying, looked, called
	- Adverb endings as needed.	luckily, proudly
RED LETTER (S)	- Identify silent letter(s). Important to remember for spelling.	one, why, know, watch, school, answered
	- May alert the reader to change the previous vowel(s) sound from a short vowel to a long vowel, or vice versa.	time, made, like, give, have
	- Guides the reader to focus on decoding the blue short/long vowel while ignoring the red vowel for vowel digraphs (two successive letters whose phonetic value is a single sound).	your, yours, could, please, people, thought, because
	- Help to distinguish the correct meaning of a homophone (Two or more words pronounced alike but are different in meaning, derivation or spelling.)	to, too, two right, write their, there hear, here

♥

I wish to dedicate this story to

the loving memory of my grandmother,

Transito Pegottini-Blatch

who encouraged me to believe in myself,

and to all the children who learn that magic begins when

they learn to believe in themselves!

♥

This story begins after the old wolf had walked many miles, up and down many hills to cross a snowy mountain peak. When he was at the top of the mountain, he was able to look down at a very beautiful valley below. He was hoping to find a foolish boy named Jack who had traded his last cow for a handful of beans. It was the end of the winter season and the snow was beginning to melt, creating rushing springs which merged into a river that ran through the middle of the valley where the farmers lived.

The old wolf delighted as he took a deep breath, inhaled the crisp mountain air and exhaled vapor from his long snout. He stopped a moment, feeling melancholic and missing his dear friends whom he had left behind. He wondered about the Little Red Hen, her three chicks that he had helped raise, the lazy dog, the sleepy cat, and the yellow duck. He really missed his old friends. However, he had to stay focused on his new mission to find Jack and his mother.

The long walk had rejuvenated his old bones and this adventure was renewing his spirits. The old wolf felt strong and energized and was most eager to reach his destination. With the valley in clear sight, he decided to follow the streams to reach the riverbank which would lead him to the valley.

It was not long before he came across three friendly billy goats who warned him about an old troll that supposedly lived under the only bridge which led to the valley. "He is a selfish and feisty old troll who doesn't let anyone cross the bridge!" complained the Little Billy Goat Gruff.

"He is a blood-thirsty mean grouch who may decide to have you for lunch!" warned the Middle Billy Goat Gruff.

"He tries to bully anyone who crosses the bridge, but he is no match for my strong horns!" proudly bragged the Big Billy Goat Gruff. The old wolf thanked the goats for their warnings and started to plan how to best deal with the upcoming situation.

The old wolf thought he could try tiptoeing across the bridge, hoping the troll would not hear his footsteps. Perhaps his old age and experience had taught the wolf a few lessons and he decided it would be best to try outsmarting the troll.

In no time at all, the old wolf was on top of the bridge shouting and howling the troll's name. "Tro...uuull! Tro...uuull!" howled the old wolf as loudly as he could.

The troll, who lived underneath the bridge, woke up from his daily afternoon nap and ran up to the bridge to find out who was howling his name so loudly. "Who dares to be on my bridge howling my name and waking me up from my afternoon nap?" shouted the troll.

"It is me the Wolf! I have come from the other side of the mountain just to repair the loose wooden planks on your bridge, Mr. Troll. I heard that some inconsiderate animals keep you awake all day and night with the clippity-clop, clippity-clop which their hooves make while stepping on the

loose wooden planks of your privately owned bridge. There is nothing worse than to be awakened from a restful and pleasant afternoon nap, especially when others are stepping across your private property making all that bothersome noise. You see, I can absolutely understand your impatience in dealing with such an annoying inconvenience. It will only take me a few minutes to nail these planks here and those planks over there on the other side of the bridge, if you would so kindly allow me to do the work," said the old wolf in a very convincing tone.

The Troll sighed, scratched his red beard, and twitched his big nose. "Old Wolf, you are lucky I am not hungry right now or I would consider having you as barbeque ribs or wolf chops for supper! On the other hand, just the look of your skinny legs tells me that you would not be much of a meal. Better get the job done fast before I change my mind!" commanded the troll.

In the blink of an eye, the old wolf grabbed a stone and hammered the loose wooden plank on one side of the bridge. Then he ran across quickly and pretended to be hammering more loose wooden planks on the opposite side. When the old wolf was clear and safe on the other side of the bridge, he hollered, "Mr. Troll, just take a good look at your old bridge. I've done such a good job that now it looks brand new!"

The troll was becoming intolerant and impatient with the old wolf and answered, "You must be a dumb wolf! How can I see the loose wooden planks? Can't you tell that I am almost blind? But I have no trouble hearing and smelling my food, especially when it walks across my bridge!"

The old wolf, no longer worried about the Troll's threats, had the audacity to ask for some food in compensation for a job well done, "Mr. Troll, now that you mention food, do you have some food to share with me?"

The grumpy troll grunted and stomped his foot, but ultimately agreed to give the old wolf some cornbread with butter and a cup of milk. The old wolf was very happy to get his first meal after such a long journey. He thanked the troll, said good-bye, and was on his way to find Jack's house.

On the road to the farm houses, he ran into Chicken Little who was in a hurry to tell the king that the sky was falling. Old Wolf stopped him to ask directions to Jack's house. Chicken Little replied, "I was just outside of Jack's window when seven small pieces of the sky fell on my head. Jack's house is small with a white picket fence and no smoke coming out of its chimney. Jack and his mother are so poor that they don't even have wood to burn in their fireplace. Just follow the Rainbow Brick Road and you will find it. Now I must hurry to tell the king that the sky is falling. Seven pieces of it fell on my head already!"

Chicken Little continued running on his way to find the king. Old Wolf took a look at him and murmured under his breath, "Look at those skinny chicken legs go! I have never

seen a chicken run so fast! Either chicken legs are getting faster, or mine are getting slower."

The old wolf took the Rainbow Brick Road and soon realized that he was totally lost. "This is what I get for following directions from a silly chicken with wild ideas about the sky falling on his head!" complained the old wolf.

Nearby, he spotted a chubby old fellow sitting on a stone wall. Old wolf thought he should ask for better directions. As the old wolf approached him, the chubby fellow became so scared and startled that he fell off the stone wall. Like an eggshell, the chubby old fellow broke into many pieces!

"Oh, no! What a dreadful mess I have gotten myself into now! I better hurry and try to re-assemble him. I've never had the patience to put puzzles together and this fellow looks like scrambled egg!" said the wolf in frustration.

Suddenly, he heard horses galloping towards him on the Rainbow Brick Road. "It is the king's horses and the king's men! I better hide before they accuse me of a crime and lock me up in the castle. I meant no harm. I just wanted clear directions and ended up scaring this poor fellow, instead. Now he is all broken. I better hide because the king's men will never believe my story!" worried the old wolf.

The men stopped and said, "Look! It is Humpty Dumpty! He must have had a great fall! He is broken and we better fix him or the king will get mad because he doesn't like to hear about things falling or breaking!" The old wolf hid behind the stone wall observing the men struggling in vain to put Humpty Dumpty together again. "These men don't have a clue how to put this Dumpty Humpty together again! Chicken Little should report *that* to the king, instead of his nonsense about the sky falling!" thought the old wolf, quickly scurrying away from the incriminating scene.

The old wolf got back on the Rainbow Brick Road and walked all the way to the end of the road. "Everything here is colored green! Either I am getting ill or I have found the lost Peridot City! I must be in the Land of Moss!" thought the old wolf. On top of the hill, he noticed a strange green mansion. The old wolf decided to knock on the huge gate. It opened by itself, inviting him to come in for a visit with the Great Warlock of Moss. "Anyone brave enough to knock on this gate will be welcome for a short visit with the great Warlock of Moss!" The voice seemed to be coming from the lion statue which was standing next to the gate.

The old wolf found this to be intriguing and exciting. He decided to investigate. "Curiosity can be very dangerous, but it may be worth the risk. I think I will check out this place. I hope it is not a trap!" he thought as he went inside.

A few moments later, he found himself in front of the great Warlock of Moss. "What has brought you to Peridot City in the Land of Moss?" asked the Warlock of Moss.

"Actually, I was on my way to find Jack's house and got lost following the Rainbow Brick Road. I need clear directions to get there, but while I am here, I would not mind learning a trick or perhaps get a treat," answered the old wolf.

"You appear to be a gentle wolf and I will grant both of your wishes. Just don't ask me for fame, fortune, or to foretell the future because they have been granted already," answered the Warlock of Moss.

Then he proceeded to show the old wolf how to do some magic tricks. After that he invited him to eat some green scrambled eggs with green catsup which was brought in by an interesting cat wearing a funny hat. The wolf had never eaten such a strange meal and a peculiar thought crossed his mind, "This meal reminds me somehow of that poor Dumpty Humpty which I left in a scrambled mess next to the Rainbow Brick Road!" Nevertheless, he ate the meal and politely thanked his host for the food and magic lessons.

Then Old Wolf asked, "Could you please draw a map to help me get to Jack's house? I must be on my way before I get more distractions."

The great Warlock of Moss replied, "Maps are outdated, my friend. This is the Twenty-first Century and you must learn to use technology instead of your brain!" He gave the old wolf a watch with a GPS wolf-navigational system which led him straight to Jack's house.

But before the old wolf left, he asked, "I have one more small favor to ask of you, Great Moss. Could you help me write a letter or send a postcard to my friends? When I was young, I did not realize the importance of going to school to learn and now I don't know how to read or write."

The Warlock of Moss eagerly agreed, "Come to my office and we will use the Internet to send emails to all of your friends!"

The wolf nervously replied, "What is this net you are talking about? The last time I saw a net, people were trying to trap animals with it!"

The Warlock of Moss laughed and said, "Relax, you outdated old wolf! Come to my office and you will learn the magic of computers and the wireless communication system called the Internet! Your friends will get your message and your picture in seconds!"

The old wolf watched with great amazement as the Warlock of Moss touched the computer keys and sent his message. How did he know the Little Red Hen's email address? That remained a secret!

The old wolf felt much better and after thanking his host, quickly left the mansion. He was so happy that he even waved good-bye to the lion statue after commanding it to open the gate. "With all this technology one no longer knows what is real and what is not!" whispered the wolf to himself as he marched away from Peridot City looking and listening in amazement to his new wolf-navigational GPS watch.

After all these events and detours, the old wolf finally arrived at his destination! He was at Jack's house and just about to knock at the front door, when he remembered what had happened at the Three Little Pig's house. He looked at the chimney and just the sight of it made his tail shiver and quiver.

He thought and thought and suddenly had a fantastic idea. "I will entice them to come out with some magic tricks! I knew the tricks I learned from the great Warlock of Moss would come in handy someday!" said the old wolf as he went around the house to Jack's window.

There on the ground he spotted the seven beans that Jack's mother had thrown out the window. Jack happened to be looking out of his window and the old wolf started to perform some magic tricks with the beans. He carefully placed two beans in a handkerchief, folded it, and started huffing and puffing. Then pronouncing some hocus-pocus words while shaking the handkerchief, two birds flew out and the beans disappeared!

Jack ran over to tell his mother, "Mom! Come here! You must see this! There is an old wolf outside my window performing magic tricks with the beans! That means the beans were indeed magical!"

"Jack, stop making up things to distract me, hoping I'll forget your punishment so you can come out of your room! I am not as foolish as you are, boy!"

But Jack insisted and his mother agreed to go outside with him to look at the old wolf's magic tricks.

The old wolf charmingly greeted Jack and his mother continuing to perform magic tricks with the beans. Jack's mother started to believe that maybe she indeed had thrown out magic beans and now she wanted them. "You must give back our beans! I threw them out thinking that they were worthless," demanded Jack's mother. "I will give them back, but without me, you will never know the secret which makes them magical", replied the old wolf.

"How can we trust you, old wolf?" said Jack's mother. "What do you want in return? You can see how poor we are and we have nothing else to give."

"I want a place I can call home for about a year. With your permission, I can stay in the hayloft and I will teach Jack how to grow the very best beans in the whole wide world. We will keep four beans to plant. We will use the other beans to make your wishes come true. Using one bean at a time, you will be allowed to make one wish every four months," the old wolf responded and Jack's mother was glad to agree.

The old wolf took out one of the beans from his pocket. He asked Jack and his mother to make a wish. Without hesitation or much thought, Jack shouted, "I wish I could grow the biggest beanstalk that would reach all the way up to the sky!"

Jack's mother was disappointed that her foolish boy had been so thoughtless, making such a silly wish in a hurry. The old wolf told Jack to plant the seed right in front of his window and go to sleep believing that his wish would come true. Jack was so excited that he did not care if he went to bed without any supper. He was happy to go to sleep, even though he was hungry, because he believed that his wish would come true.

The next morning there was a huge beanstalk right in front of Jack's window. It had grown so tall that the top reached beyond the clouds. Jack ran outside to immediately start climbing the vine. His mother ordered him to come down and, being an obedient son, he did. They went to the hayloft where the old wolf was still sleeping comfortably.

"Mr. Old Wolf! You must come down and show us how to plant the four bean seeds as you promised. Here at the farm we must start working at the crack of dawn. My foolish boy's wish came true, but one giant beanstalk won't take care of our needs and we will soon run out of

food to eat. All this foolish boy wants to do is to climb the vine. I am afraid he will fall down and break his crown," Jack's mother shouted loudly.

The old wolf woke up a bit sleepy and confused, "My lady, this is indeed a very early call, but if need be, I am a wolf of his word and your wishes and demands will be my daily commands," replied the old wolf, still groggy from a deep sleep.

Then he performed some hocus-pocus agricultural tricks. With some huffing and puffing he dug four holes in the ground where he cautiously planted the four bean seeds. Jack and his mother carefully watched how the old wolf performed his unusual planting tricks. When he was done, the old wolf told Jack, "Fetch a pail of water from the well and I will show you exactly how much water to pour over each seed, no more, no less."

Four months passed by during which Jack learned how to be a good farmer. He worked hard every morning. He climbed up the giant beanstalk every afternoon. He bragged about how high and strong the vine had grown. Using his creative imagination he started making up stories about a fe-fi-fo-fum giant who supposedly lived in a castle beyond the clouds with a wife, a singing harp, and a hen that would lay golden eggs at the giant's command.

In the meantime, the wolf harvested the beans. He took Jack and his mother to the market, showing them how to make a fair trade for the beans. Soon it was time to make the second wish. The old wolf told Jack, "This time it's your mother's turn to make a wish."

She spoke up enthusiastically, "I wish for farmers who will be willing to trade a handful of magic beans for food, a cow to give us plenty of milk and butter, and a beautiful new dress for me to wear on Sundays."

The old wolf was a bit surprised and nervously replied, "My lady, the bean is good for only one wish, not three!" Then feeling sorry for the woman, he added, "Perhaps this bean will let us stretch out your wish."

The people at the market had heard many stories about Jack's magic beans and were eager to trade anything for a handful of his beans. Their wishes came true! She went home with a wagon full of food, a beautiful new dress, and a new cow walking behind.

Time passed and Jack's magic beans became legend in the green valley. Jack had become a jolly giant in the bean trade. His mother and the old wolf became good friends. They spent every afternoon chatting and sipping chamomile tea with cookies and peanut butter sandwiches.

The old wolf was happy. He was very pleased to have new friends and to have been able to help Jack and his mother gain fame, fortune, and so many comforts. A year passed and his task was done.

The old wolf's wild instincts were telling him that it was time to depart. News was circulating about an old man named Gepetto who was very distraught about losing his marionette son named Pinocchio.

The old wolf's sense of duty called once again. His desire to feel useful inspired him to rapidly pack his few belongings.

He went to Jack's house to announce his plans for departure. "My lady, a year has already passed and it is time for me to leave. I wish to thank you for the comfortable hayloft, the food, the afternoon tea times, and the unforgettable friendships I have gained. As I promised upon my arrival, I still have the last bean for the last wish," said the old wolf taking the remaining bean from his pocket.

To his surprise, both Jack and his mother refused to take the bean to make a last wish. "Mr. Wolf, how can we ask for anything more? You have helped us gain so many things. We are forever grateful and we both insist that you keep the

magic bean for any emergency you may encounter on the road. However, we are curious to know the secret that makes the beans magical."

The old wolf replied, "The magic did not come from the beans. The magic came from your ability to believe that your wishes and dreams could come true. **Real magic begins when you learn to believe in yourself!** "

Jack and his mother had learned the best lesson! They thanked the old wolf. With sniffles and tears, they both hugged him and bid farewell to this wise old fellow who had become a true friend. The old wolf waved good-bye, saying he would come back some day.

He turned, taking a different path out of the beautiful green valley. Jack and his mother watched him lope through the fields until his silhouette grew distant and disappeared against the line of the blue horizon.

www.ingramcontent.com/pod-product-compliance
Lightning Source LLC
Chambersburg PA
CBHW041430090426
42744CB00002B/23